W

MW01710487

TREES

written by

Karen Hoenecke

KAEDEN BOOKS™

Title: We Need Trees

Author: Karen Hoenecke

ISBN: 978-1-61181-389-0

Published by:

Kaeden Corporation
P. O. Box 16190
Rocky River, Ohio 44116
1-(800)-890-READ(7323)
www.kaeden.com

Printed in the United States
W-3/2017

First edition 1998
Second edition 2002
Third edition 2007
Fourth edition 2013
Fifth edition 2014

TABLE OF CONTENTS

TREES FOR CLIMBING AND SHADE

Why do we need trees?
We need trees for climbing.

We need trees for **shade**.

TREES FOR FRUIT AND SYRUP

We need trees for fruit.

We need trees for **syrup**.

TREES FOR WOOD AND BUILDING

We need trees for wood.

We need trees for homes.

We need trees.

Glossary

shade – darkness or dimness caused by the blocking of the sun's rays or other light source

syrup – a thick, sweet liquid. Maple syrup is produced by partially boiling down the sap of the maple tree.

Index